Energy Transfer

Robert Snedden

Heinemann
LIBRARY

www.heinemann.co.uk/library
Visit our website to find out more information about Heinemann Library books.

To order:
☎ Phone 44 (0) 1865 888066
📄 Send a fax to 44 (0) 1865 314091
💻 Visit the Heinemann Library Bookshop at www.heinemann.co.uk/library to browse our catalogue and order online.

First published in Great Britain by Heinemann Library,
Halley Court, Jordan Hill, Oxford OX2 8EJ
a division of Reed Educational and Professional Publishing Ltd.
Heinemann is a registered trademark of Reed Educational & Professional Publishing Ltd.

OXFORD MELBOURNE AUCKLAND
JOHANNESBURG BLANTYRE GABORONE
IBADAN PORTSMOUTH (NH) USA CHICAGO

Designed by Celia Floyd
Illustrated by Jeff Edwards and Alan Fraser
Originated by Ambassador Litho Ltd.
Printed in Hong Kong by Wing King Tong

ISBN 0 431 11763 2 (hardback)
06 05 04 03 02 01
10 9 8 7 6 5 4 3 2 1

ISBN 0 431 11768 3 (paperback)
07 06 05 04 03 02
10 9 8 7 6 5 4 3 2 1

British Library Cataloguing in Publication Data

Snedden, Robert
  Energy transfer. – (Essential energy)
  1. Energy transfer
  I. Title
  333.7'9

Acknowledgements

The Publishers would like to thank the following for permission to reproduce photographs:
Austin J Brown/Aviation Picture Library: Pg.20; Camera Press: Pg.30, Pg.35; Corbis: Pg.5, Pg.6, Pg.9, Pg.14, Pg.24, Pg.25, Pg.29; Mary Evans Picture Library: Pg.11, Pg.21, Pg.28; Peter Gould: Pg.22; Robert Harding Picture Library: Pg.4; Science Photo Library: Pg.12, Pg.16, Pg.19, Pg.23, Pg.26, Pg.32, Pg.36, Pg.37, Pg.39, Pg.40, Pg.43.

Cover photograph reproduced with permission of Photodisc.

Every effort has been made to contact copyright holders of any material reproduced in this book. Any omissions will be rectified in subsequent printings if notice is given to the Publisher.

Any words appearing in the text in bold, **like this**, are explained in the glossary.

Contents

What is energy?

You know what it feels like to be full of energy. You feel that you could do almost anything. You feel you can make things happen. This is what energy does – 'it makes things happen'. Energy makes things move faster and makes things slow down. It makes things warmer and makes them brighter. Energy makes living things grow and thrive. The more energy there is, the more it can do.

If an object is described as energetic it means that it has the ability to do certain things. Imagine a ball sitting on the ground. It isn't very energetic because it isn't doing much. Now kick it. Suddenly it is doing things. It is moving through the air and, if you've been careless, it's just about to break a window! When you kicked the ball you gave it energy, the ability to do things.

The ball receives a transfer of energy from the foot of the person kicking it.

The working Universe

Understanding energy is about understanding how the Universe works. Indeed scientists define energy as the ability, or capacity, to do work. It comes from the Greek word *energeia*, which means 'in work'. 'Work' measures what happens as a result of transferring energy from one place to another and involves the action of a force on an object. Work is measured by multiplying the magnitude of the force by the distance moved in the direction of the force. When you kicked the ball you applied a force to it and made it move in the direction of that force.

This gives us a definition for a unit of energy. The size of a force is usually given in newtons, named after the great scientist Sir Isaac Newton. One newton is roughly the force needed to lift an average sized apple. Another way of looking at it is to say that the weight of the apple is roughly one newton. If the apple was raised to a height of one metre, the work done, or the amount of energy used, would be one joule. One joule is the work done when a force of one newton moves one metre.

Power

Energy can't move from one place to another instantaneously. Like everything else, it takes time. The rate at which energy is transferred from one place to another, or the rate at which work is being done, is called power. Power can be calculated by dividing the energy transferred by the time taken to transfer it. It is the rate at which work is done. Power is usually measured in joules per second, or watts.

A hurricane releases around 100,000 million joules of energy and so it can do a lot of damage.

Ever-changing forms

It seems that there are many different forms of energy and that energy is always being changed from one form into another. The **radiant energy** of the Sun is captured by plants and stored as **chemical energy**. Animals eat the plants and use the chemical energy to move and produce heat. The **kinetic energy** of falling water is used to produce electricity. The **electrical energy** of a lightning flash produces heat, light and sound. Perhaps a better way of looking at energy is not to think of something that keeps changing, but rather something that is transferred from one thing to another.

Energy economics

Energy is a little like having money in the bank. You can use it to do a number of things. You can transfer money to a shop, for example, by writing a cheque or by handing over cash. If you earn money it is like a flow of energy into your bank account that allows you to do more. The more you have the more you can do. Whatever method you use to transfer your money from one place to another, whether you use cash or a cheque, it still has the same value, and so it is with energy.

Plants capture the energy of sunlight, using it to power chemical reactions.

We might perceive energy in different forms, but what we are actually seeing are the effects of energy moving from one place or system to another. The energy itself is unchanged. It has not been transformed, but transferred. Although energy may appear to take on different forms, the total amount of energy present does not change. In physics, this is called the Law of Conservation of Energy and is often expressed in this way: 'Energy cannot be created or destroyed.' For example, when you turn on a light, electrical energy becomes **heat** and **light energy**, but the total amount of energy does not change.

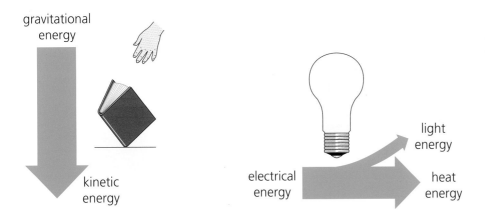

When a book falls to the ground gravitational energy turns into kinetic energy.
In a light bulb electrical energy mostly becomes heat energy with some light energy.

Energy transfers

There are a number of different ways of transferring energy from one system to another, and we shall be looking at them in this book. One way, as we have seen, is by doing work, that is causing a force to act on an object, as we do when we strike a ball with a bat. A second way to transfer energy is by heating – transferring energy from a hot object to a cold one using a temperature difference (page 10). The third way is to transfer energy by means of waves (page 32) which carry energy from one place to another.

The various forms of energy that we shall be looking at in this book, such as thermal, electrical and chemical energy, can be thought of as being the result of the kinetic energy or **potential energy** of **atoms** and **subatomic particles**. Thermal energy or heat, for example, is really a measurement of the kinetic energy of atoms. The faster the atoms are moving, the hotter the object. Electrical energy results from the motion of **electrons** through an object that conducts electricity. Chemical energy is a form of potential energy stored in the bonds that hold atoms together to form **molecules**.

Energy and movement

Physical objects may possess **kinetic energy** or **potential energy**. It is possible for an object to have both potential and kinetic energy at the same time. The hard work in riding a bike to the top of a hill is rewarded when the potential energy gained on the way up becomes kinetic energy on the way down. As you freewheel downhill the potential energy that you and your bicycle gained by climbing the hill against the force of **gravity** moment by moment becomes kinetic energy. Once you reach level ground your potential energy has been entirely changed into kinetic energy. Unless you add to your kinetic energy by peddling, eventually **friction** will slow you down and stop you as your kinetic energy becomes **heat energy**.

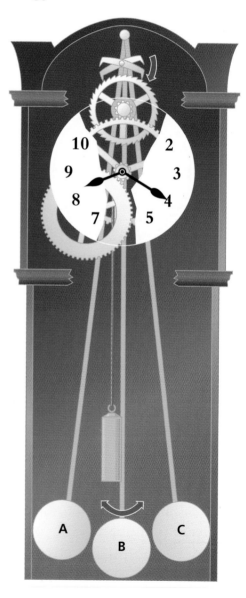

A swinging pendulum is a good illustration of the way energy changes and is conserved. At the top of its swing the pendulum's potential energy is at its maximum. At the lowest point of its swing, the pendulum has only kinetic energy. As the pendulum begins to swing back up again, kinetic energy becomes potential energy once again. However, the pendulum will not go on swinging forever. Some of the energy is lost as heat energy as a result of friction with the air. Eventually, no energy is left to do the work of lifting the pendulum.

Some clocks rely on a pendulum to keep time.

A – high point of swing

B – low point of swing

C – high point of swing

Kinetic energy and momentum

The momentum of an object is calculated by multiplying its **mass** by its **velocity**. Momentum is what makes a moving object hard to stop. The greater an object's momentum the greater the force necessary to stop it or change its direction. This means that a slow moving heavy object is just as hard to stop as a fast moving lightweight object. The kinetic energy of an object also depends on both the mass of the object and its velocity–it is linked to momentum.

Gravitational potential energy

When you lift an object up, you are working against the force of gravity by exerting a force acting in the opposite direction to gravity. The heavier the object the greater the force you have to apply to lift it. The work needed to raise the object, therefore, is equivalent to the weight of the object multiplied by the distance it is raised. The weight of the object is equal to the mass multiplied by the force of gravity. The heavier the object and the further you lift it, the greater its potential energy will be.

Elastic potential energy

An object can possess potential energy because of its state, as well as its position. When an archer pulls back the bow, elastic potential energy is being stored in the taut bowstring. When the string is released, it springs back to its original shape and the potential energy that was stored within it is transferred to the arrow, which flies forward.

Cycling uphill requires energy to resist friction and the force of gravity.

Thermodynamics

Thermodynamics is the study of the transformation of heat into and from other forms of energy. Scientists and engineers use the principles of thermodynamics for many purposes, such as designing machines and calculating how much energy is involved in a **chemical reaction**.

Internal energy

The energy contained within a substance in the form of the **kinetic** and **potential energy** of the particles that make it up is called its **internal energy**. The hotter an object is, the higher its level of internal energy. A substance's temperature is really a measure of its internal energy. When a substance changes from one state to another, for example when solid ice changes to liquid water, the particles in the liquid are moving around much more than they do in the solid. In their new state the water molecules have a higher internal energy.

Heat is energy transferred as a result of a temperature difference. It is the movement of energy from a region of high internal energy to a region of low internal energy. When you put ice in a drink, heat flows from the drink to the ice, melting it. The internal energy of the ice increases due to the transfer of heat, and the internal energy of the drink becomes less. Like any other form of energy, internal energy can be transferred from place to place, but it cannot be created or destroyed.

Heat and work

Work is energy transferred by forces when they move and heat is energy transferred due to a temperature difference. Heat and mechanical work can be changed from one into the other. James Prescott Joule (1818–89) demonstrated that it is possible to raise the temperature of a substance by doing work on it, in the same way that the temperature can be raised by heating. Stirring a liquid, for example, causes its temperature to rise. Joule called the idea that mechanical work gave rise to a temperature change the 'mechanical equivalent of heat'. Today we measure all forms of energy, including heat, using the same unit, the joule, named in honour of James Joule's work.

James Prescott Joule (1818–89), born in Salford, Lancashire, was one of the first people to realize that heat was a form of energy and that work produced heat. As the son of a wealthy brewer he could afford to devote himself to a life of research. Even on his honeymoon he carried out an experiment that showed that the water at the bottom of a waterfall was warmer than the water at the top because its kinetic energy became heat energy.

First law of thermodynamics

Joule's work formed the basis for what became the first law of thermodynamics. According to this law, if you measure all of the energy present in a closed space (or 'closed system' as physicists call it) before and after something happens, you will find that the total amount of energy remains the same at the end as it was at the beginning. However, some of it may have changed form (for example, kinetic energy may have changed into heat). The first law says that:

> 'The change in a system's internal energy is equal to the heat absorbed from the surroundings minus the work done on the surroundings.'

In thermodynamics the behaviour of a system must always be seen in relationship to its surroundings. The Universe as a whole could be thought of as a system without (so far as we know!) any surroundings. Therefore, the total amount of energy present in the Universe remains the same, as there is no way to add or subtract energy from the Universe, leading us to the law of the conservation of energy.

Entropy and the arrow of time

As we have seen, heat flows from a region of high **internal energy** to a region of low internal energy. It never goes in the opposite direction.

Second law of thermodynamics

The second law of **thermodynamics** deals with the natural direction of energy processes and can be stated in a number of ways. For example, according to this law, heat will, of its own accord, flow only from a hotter object to a colder object. German professor of physics Rudolf Clausius (1822–88) said: 'Heat cannot of itself pass from a colder to a hotter body.' Lord Kelvin (1824–1907) put the law like this:

> 'It is impossible to derive mechanical effect by cooling a body below the temperature of the coldest of the surrounding bodies.'

In other words, you can't do work by using up heat from the coldest part of a system.

This under-floor insulation is being installed under the floorboards of a house to help keep the heat from escaping.

Time's arrow

Thermodynamic systems have another property, distinct from energy, that is related to the amount of useful work that can be obtained from the system. This property is called **entropy**. Systems with low entropy possess relatively more energy capable of being converted to useful work. In most natural processes entropy always increases, meaning that less energy is available to do useful work. For example, if a car brakes, the **kinetic energy** of the car is transferred to **heat energy** which is then dissipated and can perform no useful task.

The second law of thermodynamics shows that physical processes happen in one direction. Sometimes this is called the 'arrow of time', pointing the way from the past into the future. So there is another way the second law of thermodynamics can be given:

'No process is possible in which there is an overall decrease in the entropy of the Universe.'

This means it is impossible to move heat from one system at a lower temperature to another at a higher temperature because to do so would result in a decrease in the overall entropy.

Entropy and chemistry

Chemical reactions that involve a change from an ordered arrangement of **molecules** to an arrangement that is more disordered or random are more likely to occur because the random arrangement has a lower level of energy available to do work. An increase in randomness means an increase in entropy, which again is in line with the second law of thermodynamics. To go in the opposite direction, from a situation where there is a great deal of randomness to one that is ordered, requires an input of energy.

A tree is a very ordered structure, so it is low in entropy. The tree's cells had to capture a great deal of the Sun's energy to make the wood and other materials that form it from disordered carbon dioxide, water and other molecules. Burning that wood releases energy and increases the level of entropy as the wood is reduced to ash and gas.

Perpetual motion

A perpetual motion machine is a machine that can run forever without any outside energy input. You never have to push it, refuel it or wind it up. Once it starts, it just keeps on going. This sounds too good to be true – and it is. There are no perpetual motion machines at the moment – only ideas!

Conservation of energy

There is a very good reason why there can be no perpetual motion. It is one of the basic laws of physics: the law of the conservation of energy. Expanded energy is always lost from a system, and cannot be recovered. Energy can be changed from one form to another, but according to the conservation law it can never be created or destroyed. For example, an aircraft will only keep flying for as long as it has fuel. The **chemical energy** of the fuel is turned into **heat energy** as it is burned and this heat becomes thrust to power the aircraft forward. If the fuel runs out, the aircraft falls to the ground. (Incidentally, the falling aircraft is still converting energy, the **potential energy** it has gained from its height is converted to **kinetic energy** as it plunges to the ground!)

A satellite in orbit around the Earth would seem to be in perpetual motion. However, it is continually converting potential energy from the Earth's **gravity** into kinetic energy as it orbits.

Friction

Friction is the resistance you feel whenever you rub one thing against another. Friction changes **mechanical energy** into heat energy. Even the aircraft moving through the air creates friction as it pushes aside the air **molecules**. Every machine, no matter how smooth or well oiled, will always produce some friction. Some of the machine's mechanical energy is always lost as friction changes it to heat energy.

Heat energy

The heat energy would be no good for the perpetual motion machine either because of the second law of **thermodynamics**, which says that heat energy always flows from a warm body to a cold body. Some of the heat energy produced by a machine is always going to escape to the colder, outside air.

You can convert one kind of energy to another but you cannot end up with more energy than you started with. This is what a perpetual motion machine would be doing. It would be making energy out of nothing.

Keep on trying!

The United States Patent Office receives about a hundred applications each year for devices that involve some form of perpetual motion. Applications must be accompanied by a working model!

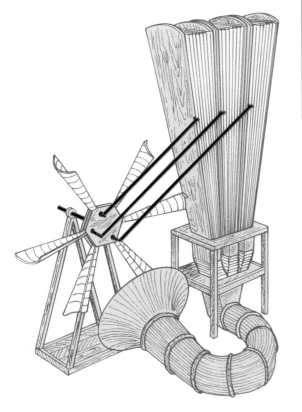

This idea for a perpetual motion machine uses the windmill to power the bellows, which create wind to turn the windmill. But it will not work because no matter how hard a push you give it, eventually all of its mechanical energy will be converted to heat by friction and the machine will stop.

Zero energy

Is it possible to arrive at a state in which there is no energy available at all? At **absolute zero**, the coldest possible temperature, all **atoms** and **molecules** are motionless. This temperature represents a complete absence of energy. There is nowhere in the Universe that is at this temperature, even the dust between the stars is at a few degrees above absolute zero.

Absolute temperature

The absolute temperature scale is the temperature scale commonly used by scientists. It is also known as the Kelvin scale of temperature as it was first proposed by Lord Kelvin. Its unit is the kelvin (K) and the scale starts at 0K, or absolute zero. It is not possible to have a temperature that is lower than this. A 1K increase in temperature represents the same increase as a 1°C increase. On the Kelvin scale, the melting point of ice is 273.15K and the boiling point of water is 373.15K (100°C).

Dry ice is solid carbon dioxide. It sublimes (changes straight into a gas from the solid state) at −78.5°C (195°K).

There are three commonly-used temperature scales, shown here with a few key transitional temperatures.

0°	93°	273°	373°
Kelvin			
−273°	−180°	0°	100°
Celsius			
−459°	−292°	32°	212°
Fahrenheit			
absolute zero	oxygen becomes liquid	ice melts	water boils

The third law of thermodynamics

The third law of **thermodynamics** states that the **entropy** of a substance approaches zero as its temperature approaches absolute zero.

Although absolute zero is experimentally unobtainable, it has been approached to within a few billionths of a degree. What the third law means in practice is that we can never actually reach absolute zero in a fixed number of operations. The closer we get to absolute zero, the harder it gets to go any further. You can see that this must be so when you recall that heat can only flow from a region of high temperature to a region of lower temperature. In order to cool an object there must be an even cooler object into which its heat can flow.

Experiments with gases

Absolute zero was deduced from experiments with gases. It was found that the pressure of a gas would rise and fall as its temperature rose and fell. By plotting a graph of temperature against pressure, and then extending the line back to zero pressure, absolute zero can be found.

The zeroth law

The zeroth law of thermodynamics does not have anything to do with absolute zero. It was developed in the 1930s, after the other thermodynamics laws, but it is called the Zeroth Law because it comes logically before the first and second laws. It can be stated like this:

'Two objects (or systems) that are in thermal equilibrium (at the same temperature) with a third object (or system) must be in thermal equilibrium with each other.'

It is sometimes called the 'baby in the bath rule'. A parent will dip an elbow into the bathwater to test the temperature before putting a baby in. If the elbow is in equilibrium with the water and the parent is in equilibrium with the baby, then it follows that the baby is in equilibrium with the water. There will be no flow of heat from one to the other when the baby is placed in the bath, and so no yells of protest!

Heat flows

Heat energy can be transferred in three different ways: by conduction, by convection and by **radiation**.

Conduction

This is the means by which heat energy is transferred through solids. Some materials are better at conducting than others. If you leave a metal spoon in a hot liquid it becomes hot to the touch, while a wooden spoon does not. The reason for this can be found in the way the **atoms** and **molecules** are arranged in each substance.

When something is heated the particles from which it is made gain **kinetic energy**. They start to bump up against each other, transferring energy as they do so. In a metal there is a sea of freely moving **electrons** surrounding a framework of positively charged metal **ions**. If one part of the metal is heated, the ions there begin to vibrate more as they gain energy. Electrons pick up kinetic energy from the ions as they collide with them, then as they travel through the framework, they collide with other ions and electrons, passing kinetic energy on to them. In this way, the heat energy applied at one point is passed on quickly to other parts of the metal.

In non-**conductors**, such as wood, there are no freely moving particles to transfer energy. Instead, the energy is transferred through the forces that hold the particles together and this is a much slower process.

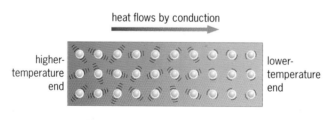

heat flows by conduction

higher-temperature end

lower-temperature end

Heat flow by conduction.

Convection

Convection is the means by which heat is transferred through a fluid. As a liquid or a gas is heated, it expands and becomes less dense. The less dense part of the fluid rises and is replaced beneath by the cooler, denser part of the fluid, which is heated in its turn. In this way, a convection current is set up with fluid rising from the source of heat, cooling, sinking down and being heated again.

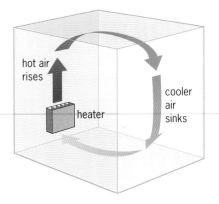

hot air rises

heater

cooler air sinks

A heater heats the air in a room in the same way – through convection currents.

Radiation

Objects that are hotter than their surroundings radiate energy in the form of **electromagnetic energy**. As the temperature of an object increases, so too does the range of **frequencies** of electromagnetic energy that it emits. If an item such as a metal rod is heated it will first glow dull red, then orange and eventually glow white hot as it radiates light at all **wavelengths**. The light given off by a hot object is called **incandescence**.

A strip of steel glows bright yellow in a steel mill.

Heat engines

Mechanical energy and **heat energy** are related, as James Joule showed. An engine works on the principle that a gas will expand when it is heated. The burning fuel heats a gas and the force of the expanding gas is harnessed to drive the machinery. Engines can be classified according to whether they burn their fuel inside the engine (internal combustion engine, such as an automobile or jet engine) or outside the engine (external combustion engine, such as a steam engine).

The engines of a jet aircraft convert the **chemical energy** of aviation fuel into **kinetic energy**, sound and heat.

Heat into motion

A steam turbine is one example of an external combustion engine. Heat is produced by burning a **fossil fuel** or from **nuclear energy** in a nuclear reactor. This is used to change water in a boiler to steam at high temperature, causing it to expand greatly. Pipes direct the high-pressure steam on to the bladed wheels of the turbine, which are attached to a shaft. The spinning shaft can be used to do useful work, such as turning the propeller on a submarine or driving an electricity generator. The steam leaving the turbine has a much lower temperature and is collected in a condenser where it can be turned into water again (condensed) and recycled back to the boiler.

The petrol engine and diesel engines that power many vehicles are examples of internal combustion engines. The fuel is sprayed into the cylinders of the engine where a spark in the petrol engine, or hot compressed air in the diesel engine, makes it explode, forming a vapour of hot gases. The gases expand and push down pistons in the cylinders. The motion of the pistons moves the crankshaft that turns a set of gearwheels in the gearbox, which rotates a driveshaft that turns the car's wheels.

Engines and efficiency

The study of **thermodynamics** really began in the 19th century when the French engineer Sadi Carnot (1796–1832) set out 'to determine mathematically how much work can be got out of a steam engine'. Carnot's most important finding was that it is not possible for an engine to be 100 per cent efficient.

Steam engines were used for many tasks, such as lifting coal from mineshafts.

The engine cannot convert all of the heat energy from its fuel into mechanical energy because inevitably some energy is lost as heat to colder objects around it. For example, in a power station some of the energy from the fuel used to heat water and turn it into steam will also heat the vessel the water is contained in. This energy cannot be used to do work and so is lost.

Any engine that uses heat to do work needs to have a low temperature 'sink', as it is called, for heat to be transferred to, otherwise the engine will simply not work. The low temperature sink draws the heat energy from the source. Because the sink is heated in the process, it follows that all of the energy produced by the source can never be used to do useful work. In a steam engine, for example, the condenser acts as the heat sink.

Chemical energy

Some **chemical reactions** take place very slowly, such as iron combining with oxygen in the presence of water to form rust. Others are very swift, such as the sudden burst of sound and light that comes when a firework explodes.

For chemicals to react together, the **molecules** that make them up must be on the move so that the **reactants** can come into contact with each other. If the collision takes place with sufficient energy to break the bonds holding the molecules together, then new compounds can be formed.

This torch uses the stored **chemical energy** of batteries.

Exothermic and endothermic reactions

All molecules have a certain amount of **potential energy**. This energy is the sum of all the chemical bonds in the molecule. Knowing how much energy is stored in substances helps to determine how easily a chemical reaction will take place. When a chemical reaction takes place the energy equation has to balance. An exothermic reaction is one in which energy is released, usually in the form of heat. The energy stored in the molecules produced by the reaction, plus the energy released, is equal to the energy stored in the reactants.

An endothermic reaction is one in which heat is taken in from the surroundings. **Photosynthesis** is an example of an endothermic reaction. Green plants use energy from sunlight to make sugars from carbon dioxide and water.

For obvious reasons exothermic reactions are more likely to take place than endothermic reactions. In fact, most chemical reactions produce heat. According to the second law of **thermodynamics** the total energy present in a system will remain constant; however, following a chemical reaction the total amount of potential energy in the system will be less than at the beginning. All chemical reactions lead to a change in the type of energy present, resulting in an overall loss of potential energy.

Making and breaking bonds

A chemical reaction is a two-step process. In order for it to happen the bonds that hold **atoms** together in molecules have to be broken and then reformed in a different way. Breaking the bonds that hold atoms together requires energy, so the first stage of the process is always endothermic. When the new bonds are formed energy is released. If the energy released is greater than the energy that was needed to break the original bonds then the reaction is exothermic. If the energy released is less than was originally needed then the reaction is endothermic.

The energy that is needed to start a reaction off is called the activation energy. The smaller the activation energy required, the more rapidly will the reaction proceed.

The sound and light of a fireworks display results from a series of highly energetic chemical reactions.

Energy in the living world

The living world can be thought of as an energy-based economy with plants and some **micro-organisms** as the producers of the energy, converting it from the Sun's energy, and all other living things as **consumers** of that energy. Energy is passed from organism to organism along a **food chain**. Less energy is available at every link in the chain as it is transformed into unusable forms such as heat and indigestible tissues.

Grazing cows make use of some of the energy the grass originally captured from the Sun.

Life and thermodynamics

Living organisms are highly organized and could be considered as low **entropy** systems. To maintain their order, organisms need nutrients and a continuous supply of energy. They also need to be able to create a lot of disorder outside themselves so as not to upset the second law of **thermodynamics**! Entropy must never decrease overall. Respiration, the process by which living things obtain their energy, creates disorder, as large **molecules**, such as glucose, are broken down into smaller, less ordered molecules of carbon dioxide and water.

Photosynthesis is not a particularly efficient way of capturing energy. Plants only trap between 1 and 3 per cent of the **solar energy** that reaches them.

Primary production

The living economy needs to get its energy from somewhere and for the vast majority of living things that source of energy is ultimately the Sun. Organisms, such as green plants, that can capture the energy of the Sun directly are called autotrophs, which means 'self-feeders'. Through the process of **photosynthesis**, autotrophs use the Sun's energy to turn carbon dioxide and water into larger molecules. Some of these molecules are used to build new plant material and some are used in respiration to provide the plant with energy.

Energy flow

In a living community organisms occupy what are called **trophic levels**. Trophic means feeding and so a trophic level is the position in the community at which the organism feeds. Autotrophs feed themselves. Animals that eat the autotrophs are called **herbivores** and animals that eat the herbivores are called **carnivores**. There can be more than one level of carnivore, with big carnivores such as killer whales, eating smaller carnivores such as seals.

Energy is passed from one trophic level to the next, and at every level energy is lost to the community. Approximately 90 per cent of the energy at one level is lost to the level above. In other words, only about 10 per cent of the energy captured by the plants ends up producing herbivores, and about 10 per cent of the energy captured by herbivores ends up producing carnivores. Of course much depends on factors such as how much of the plant material is actually consumed by the herbivores and how efficient they are at converting what they eat into new herbivore tissues.

The lioness is a top-level carnivore. She gets her energy by eating herbivores who obtained their energy from eating plants.

Chains, webs and pyramids

Food chains are a way of showing the routes taken by energy and materials as they move through a living community, or ecosystem, from producers (mainly plants) through a series of **consumers** (**herbivores** and then **carnivores**). At every stage some of the energy goes to the decomposer community (such as certain fungi and bacteria) in the form of waste products or in the uneaten remains of a plant or animal.

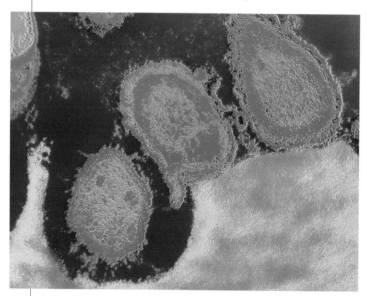

Bacteria in a cow's stomach get their energy by digesting some of the plant material the cow swallows. Cows cannot digest this material themselves – without the bacteria they would starve!

Food webs show what the organisms in an ecosystem eat and what they are eaten by. A web is made up of a collection of interlinked food chains, and illustrates the different pathways that energy and nutrients may take through the community. The links between chains may be complicated and variable.

Following the chains

Food chains are a very simple representation of what happens in living communities. At one end of a food chain there will be a plant. During **photosynthesis** the plant captures energy from the Sun. Some of this energy is passed to consumers when the plant is eaten by an animal, such as an insect. If the insect is eaten by a bird some of the energy the insect has obtained from the plant is passed to the bird. When the bird dies some of the energy will be taken by decomposers such as fungi and bacteria. However, it is not likely that the plant will be eaten by just one insect, or the insect by just one bird.

Making the picture still more complicated are animals such as ourselves, called omnivores, that eat both plants and animals. In addition, animals may switch from one chain to another depending on food supply, so that the food chains can vary over time. As a result, the food chain may have many branches, linking it to other food chains and the whole picture of links between living things in the community forms a food web.

kingfisher

Pyramids of energy

As we have seen, energy is lost at every link in the food chain. The result is that the number of organisms that can be supported at each level is reduced. This drop in numbers at each level forms a pyramid of numbers. Another way of looking at it is to say that the total **mass** of the organisms at each level decreases. This is called a pyramid of biomass. This is a better way of looking at, for example, a single oak tree that may be providing food for a vast army of insects and other animals.

perch

shrimp

Ecologists sometimes use pyramids of energy to illustrate the flow of energy from one **trophic level** to the next. From the law of conservation of energy it should be obvious that the upper levels of the pyramid must be smaller than the levels beneath them. No more energy can be made available for the herbivores than has been captured by the producers, and the carnivores have no more energy available than they can obtain by consuming the herbivores.

zooplankton (animal plankton)

phytoplankton (plant plankton)

Sun

In this example of a simple food chain the phytoplankton are the autotrophs and so become the producers. The end consumer (and carnivore) is the kingfisher.

Electrical energy

Electricity is a form of energy that affects our lives in many ways. It is a result of the existence of electrical charge. All matter is composed of **atoms**, which are made up of **subatomic particles**. Two of those particles, **electrons** and **protons**, possess a property called 'charge'. Electrons have a negative charge and protons have a positive charge. Particles with the same charge repel one another, while particles with the opposite charge attract one another. In ordinary circumstances an atom will have the same number of protons as electrons (the charges are in balance) and so the atom is neutral, meaning it has no overall charge. Sometimes electrons are pulled free from atoms, creating an overall negative charge in one place and an overall positive charge in another. This happens if you rub a balloon on a woollen sweater. Electrons are transferred from one to the other, resulting in static electricity.

Electric currents

If negative and positive charges are separated, an electrical **potential energy** is created. This potential is also called voltage, and it represents the amount of work it would take to move the charge between two points. The volt is a measure of the potential energy of the source or the 'pressure' pushing electrons through a **conductor**.

If separated electric charges are allowed to move, they create an electric current. An electric current consists of charged particles (most often electrons) moving through a conductor. The electrons in metals are free to move from one atom to another and so metals are excellent conductors. Materials, such as plastics, which do not contain freely moving electrons, are called **insulators**.

Michael Faraday (1791–1867), one of the world's greatest scientists and inventor of the electric motor and the transformer.

When an electric current moves continuously in one direction, it is called a direct current. Direct current is produced by a battery as a result of **chemical reactions** taking place between the positive and negative electrodes. The generators that produce the electricity in power stations are called alternators because they produce alternating current. Alternating current switches direction many times a second.

The amount of electric current flowing in a wire is measured in amperes, or amps. One amp is equal to about six billion billion electrons per second. Electric power, or the speed at which an electric current can do work, is measured in watts. Watts multiplied by time gives the amount of energy an electrical appliance uses to do work. In everyday speech we usually refer to these units as 'watts' when in fact they are really watt-hours. For example, a 100-watt light bulb operating for one hour uses 100 watts of energy. Electricity used in the home is usually measured in kilowatt-hours or thousands of watt-hours.

Workers in a power plant standing beside a generator gives some idea of the size of the equipment used there.

Electricity and magnetism

The connection between electricity and magnetism was discovered in the early part of the 19th century. In 1820 Hans Christian Øersted found that a wire carrying an electric current deflects the needle of a magnetic compass. The reason it does so is because a magnetic field is created by the moving electric charges that make up the current.

Following Øersted's discovery, the various magnetic effects of an electric current were investigated by other scientists. In 1831 Michael Faraday and Joseph Henry independently discovered that a current could be produced in a conductor by changing the magnetic field around it. This effect, called electromagnetic induction, together with the discovery that an electric current produces a magnetic field, opened the way for the development of the generator, which produces electricity, and the electric motor, which converts **electrical energy** into **kinetic energy**.

Electromagnetic spectrum

A regularly changing electric current in a **conductor** will create a changing magnetic field in the space around the conductor, which in turn gives rise to a changing electrical field. These interacting electric and magnetic fields can be visualized as waves travelling through space at right angles to one another and to the direction of travel of the energy. This idea of **electromagnetic radiation** was developed by James Clerk Maxwell in the middle of the 19th century.

Electromagnetic radiation is the only form of energy that can travel through the **vacuum** of space. All other forms of energy, such as **electrical energy**, heat and sound, have to be transmitted through a physical medium.

Maxwell showed that electromagnetic radiation can be thought of as waves travelling through space at the speed of light, roughly 300,000 kilometres a second. There are an infinite variety of these forms of energy, varying in their **wavelengths** and **frequencies**.

Hot objects give off infrared radiation. Cameras that are sensitive to infrared radiation have been linked to this computer to help pinpoint forest fires.

The complete range of wavelengths is called the electromagnetic spectrum. A tiny band of this range of wavelengths is seen by us as visible light. The shortest waves are the high-energy gamma rays and the longest are low-energy radio waves. Very low frequency radio waves can measure nearly 10 kilometres from crest to crest. In order of decreasing wavelength and increasing frequency, various types of electromagnetic radiation include: radio waves (including AM, FM and shortwaves), microwaves, infrared, visible light, ultraviolet, X-rays, and gamma **radiation**.

Light

Visible light is just a small part of the electromagnetic spectrum, but light represents a large portion of the total energy emitted by the Sun. In fact, 42 per cent of the **solar energy** that reaches the Earth consists of visible light. The light that is detected by the human eye has wavelengths from 0.75 to 0.40 micrometres (1 micrometre equals 0.001 millimetre). Humans perceive different wavelengths of the visible spectrum as different colours. Red light has the longest wavelength and violet the shortest. The combination of all colours is seen as white light.

Giving out light

Objects may emit light in two ways. Thermal radiation, or **incandescence**, is a consequence of an object's temperature. Generally, the hotter something gets the whiter the light it gives off. Luminescence is produced by **chemical reactions** and can result when a substance is exposed to bombardment by **electrons**, electromagnetic radiation or electric fields. Energy from any of these sources may be absorbed by certain **atoms**, which then release the energy again as light.

Fluorescence, common in many rocks, is a result of the emission of light when atoms are excited by certain types of radiation, especially ultraviolet. A familiar example is a clock or watch face that glows in the dark after it has been exposed to light. Phosphorescence is a similar process, resulting either from the absorption of light or from chemical reactions.

Waves

Other forms of energy are transmitted by waves, including sound waves, and physical waves such as ocean waves. Sound and electromagnetic waves are usually rhythmic, which means that they have a repeating pattern, but waves may also be brief, nonrepeating bursts, such as the shock wave from an explosion.

Transverse and longitudinal waves

In transverse waves, individual particles move **perpendicular** to the direction of the advancing waves. Water waves are transverse, as is all **electromagnetic radiation**. As a water wave moves forward, the water moves up and down at right angles to the direction of the wave. The vibration in longitudinal waves is in the same direction as the wave is travelling. These waves cause particles to **oscillate** along a line in the direction the waves are moving. Sound waves are longitudinal waves. As the wave passes through the air **molecules** repeatedly move together and apart producing regions of high and low pressure.

Wave properties

A wave is a disturbance that moves through a medium without causing the medium itself to move significantly. Waves carry both **potential** and **kinetic energy**, and matter is displaced as the wave passes, but no particle carrying the wave ever moves far from its original position. For example, a log floating on the sea will simply bob up and down as a wave passes it. It won't be swept forward. The shape of a wave, or the waveform, shows how the energy changes as the wave passes.

The amount by which matter is moved at any point in a wave is called its displacement. The greatest displacement is equal to the amplitude of the wave. The **velocity** of a wave is not affected by its amplitude. The greater the amplitude of a wave, the more energy it transmits. For example, a sound wave with a large amplitude will be louder than one with a small amplitude.

Amplitude is the height of a crest, or depth of a trough. Wavelength is the distance betwen the same point on successive waves.

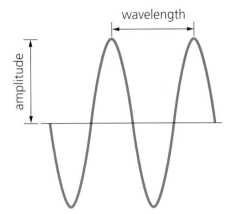

The period of a wave is the time it takes for one complete wave oscillation to occur. If ten wave crests pass a point in one second, the period would be 0.1 second. **Frequency** is the number of complete waves (or oscillations) that occur over a given time period. Frequency is usually measured in cycles per second, or Hertz (Hz) after physicist Heinrich Hertz. Hertz discovered radio waves in 1888 when he noticed that a large spark caused a small spark to jump across a gap in a coil of wire on the other side of the room. Radio waves generated by the large spark had produced electricity in the wire. A frequency of 100 Hz is equal to 100 cycles per second; a megahertz (mHz) is a million cycles per second.

Interference

The degree of movement produced by a wave at any point is called its phase. As it goes from crest to trough and back again the phase is constantly changing. When two waves overlap, a phenomenon called interference results. The crests of two waves of the same frequency arriving together are said to be 'in phase'. If the crests and troughs of the two waves coincide, they will reinforce each other and produce a wave with a larger amplitude. If the crest of one wave coincides with the trough of the other, the two waves may cancel each other. These waves are said to be 'out of phase'. Light waves are brighter in phase and darker out of phase. Sound waves are louder or softer in and out of phase.

Packets of energy

Electromagnetic energy has a rather odd property – sometimes it acts like a wave; at other times it seems to act as if it were a stream of particles.

In a speech given to the German Physical Society on 19 October 1900, Max Planck suggested that light, heat and other forms of **radiation** exists in packets, or particles, rather than being a continuous quality that could be divided into smaller and smaller parts. He called these packets of energy 'quanta' (singular **quantum**). Scientists came to think of single bundles of electromagnetic energy as particles called **photons**. Just as if they were waves, each photon can be thought of as having a **frequency**. The higher its frequency, the more energy the photon carries. In fact it has been shown that all **subatomic particles** behave as if they were both waves and particles.

Photoelectric effect

An important illustration of the above is the photoelectric effect. Light shining on certain materials will knock **electrons** loose from **atoms** (this is the principle behind **photovoltaic cells**, which turn the energy of sunlight into electricity). Albert Einstein proposed that a precise amount of energy was required to knock an electron loose from its orbit. A photon of a certain frequency or higher, that is one that had enough energy, could knock an electron loose. The electron would fly off with a **kinetic energy** that was equal to the energy of the photon minus the energy that was needed to knock the electron from the atom. This was confirmed by experiments.

Each electron around an atom has a certain 'energy state'. An electron can move to a higher energy state only by absorbing a precise amount, or quantum, of energy. An electron can drop to a lower state by giving out energy in the form of a photon. An electron moving from one energy state to another is said to make a 'quantum leap'. This is what happens in **fluorescence**. Atoms of a fluorescent material absorb energy from ultraviolet light and some of the electrons jump up to higher energy states. Some of the electrons then fall back to lower levels, releasing photons of visible light as they do so.

Photons and lasers

A laser makes use of the fact that an atom will emit a photon of radiation when one of its electrons drops to a lower energy state. ('Laser' stands for Light Amplification by Stimulated Emission of Radiation.) A simple laser is made from a tube filled with gas or liquid or a rod of transparent crystal. A mirror is placed at one end of the tube or rod and a half-silvered mirror at the other. Energy is added to the laser either by shining another light source into it, by adding electrical energy or by means of a **chemical reaction**. This raises electrons in the laser to higher energy states.

Some of the electrons fall back to a lower state, emitting photons as they do so. The photons that travel toward the sides of the laser are lost, but those travelling along the length of the rod or tube are reflected back by the mirrors. When they strike other excited atoms, they stimulate those atoms to release photons of the exact same energy level (or **wavelength**). Laser light is of single wavelength because the photon wavelength is determined by the characteristics of the atoms in the material used to make the laser. An intense, highly-focused beam of light is produced from the half-silvered end of the laser. Because it travels in a tight beam, laser light can carry a large amount of energy over a great distance.

Laser can be used to create fabulous large-scale effects, like this outdoor display which was part of the millennium celebrations in London.

Energy and mass

In his theory of relativity, Albert Einstein put forward the idea of a relationship between **mass** and energy. If an object is accelerated, whether it is an atomic particle or a spaceship, energy has to be used. As the object goes faster, its mass increases. This means that ever more energy is needed to accelerate it further. If the object were to travel as fast as the speed of light, its mass would become infinite. It is impossible to accelerate something to the speed of light because it would take an infinite amount of energy to do so.

Einstein showed the connection between mass and energy mathematically. Energy has mass, and mass represents energy. Sometimes mass is referred to as 'rest-energy', as it is energy at rest. The relationship is expressed in the equation: $E = mc^2$, where c is the speed of light.

Since c is a very large number, even a very small amount of mass represents a very large amount of energy. For example, in

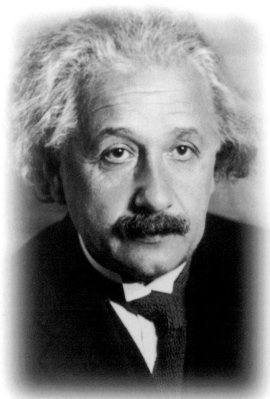

nuclear bombs and power plants, mass is converted to energy by either fission or fusion reactions. In nuclear fission, an **atom** of a heavy element, such as uranium, splits into two or more smaller atoms. The mass of the smaller atoms adds up to less than the mass of the original uranium atom, and the difference is released as energy. In fusion, two atoms of a very light element, such as hydrogen, join to form an atom of a heavier element, usually helium. Again, the mass of the resulting atom is less than the total mass of the original atoms, and energy is released. It is this process that takes place inside stars such as the Sun, resulting in tremendous amounts of energy being produced. Every second, the Sun turns four million tonnes of its mass into energy!

Albert Einstein (1879–1955). His ideas helped to open the way for the development of nuclear power.

Mass-energy conservation

The theory of relativity replaced the old ideas that mass and energy could not be created or destroyed with the new concept of the conservation of mass-energy. We might think of mass as being a form of energy, or of energy as having mass. When you kick a ball you actually increase its mass by a very tiny amount as a result of the **kinetic energy** you give it. If you leave a hot drink to cool it loses mass as it cools. A cup of cold coffee is about 0.00000000000001 kilograms lighter than a cup of hot coffee! These changes really only become obvious at speeds approaching that of light. For example, an **electron** accelerated to near light speed in a particle accelerator becomes more than 40,000 times heavier than it would be ordinarily.

In 1939, with World War II approaching, Einstein was persuaded by fellow scientists to write a letter to American President Roosevelt urging the US to begin a programme of nuclear research. Scientists in Berlin had just discovered the fissioning of uranium and Einstein's letter drew the President's attention to the 'extremely powerful bombs' that might be made by harnessing the energy released by fission. This led to the Manhattan Project, which developed the atom bombs that exploded over Hiroshima and Nagasaki in 1945. Some people have blamed the atom bomb on Einstein because he discovered the relation between mass and energy, but he took no part in the Manhattan Project and was horrified by its results.

Matter is converted into energy in the awesome explosion of a hydrogen bomb.

Nuclear energy

An **atom** can be divided into two parts. First there is an outer cloud of tiny particles called **electrons**. The number of electrons in the outermost part of this cloud determine how the atom will react with other atoms in **chemical reactions**. Electrons can be shared or transferred from one atom to another, forming chemical bonds that hold atoms together in **molecules**.

Inside the electron cloud is the nucleus of the atom. This consists of a tightly packed cluster of particles called **protons** and **neutrons**. Protons have a positive charge and, because they are so close together in the nucleus, there is a powerful repulsive electric force between them. This would cause the atom to fly apart if it were not for a stronger attractive force called the 'strong nuclear force'. All stable nuclei have at least as many neutrons as protons and larger nuclei have many more neutrons than protons. The protons and neutrons take no part in chemical reactions.

The central nucleus of an atom, made up of clusters of protons and neutrons, is surrounded by orbiting electrons.

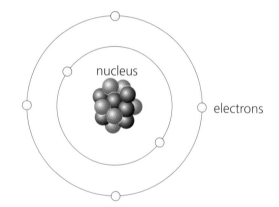

nucleus

electrons

Radioactive elements

Of the known elements, 92 are known to occur in nature, those with atomic numbers from 1 (hydrogen) to 92 (uranium). Eighty-one of these elements are stable; all the others are radioactive. A radioactive substance is one in which the nuclei of its atoms are unstable. The protons and neutrons are not so tightly bound as they are in stable atoms. The nucleus **decays**, emitting atomic particles or **electromagnetic radiation**, forming a nucleus that is more stable than it was before. A radioactive element may go through several stages of decay before finally becoming a stable element.

Every time a nucleus decays, energy is released because the total **masses** of the new nucleus and the particles are less than the mass of the original nucleus. If the atom is split by nuclear fission, the amount of energy released is massive. It amounts to 50 million times more energy per atom than can be obtained by burning carbon in the form of **fossil fuels**. Taking into account the fact that uranium atoms are much more massive than carbon atoms, it still means that a given mass of uranium can provide 2.5 million times more energy than would be obtained by burning the same mass of carbon.

Most of the energy is in the form of **kinetic energy** as the nucleus flies apart. This kinetic energy is rapidly converted into **heat energy** as the fragments of the nucleus collide with other atoms. This heat can be used to generate electricity in a nuclear power station. Some of the remaining energy is carried off in the form of radioactivity.

Half-life

There is no way to predict when any one radioactive nucleus will decay. However, it is possible to say that half of the atoms in a particular sample of a radioactive material will have decayed by a certain time. This is called the radioactive element's half-life. These can range from a tiny fraction of a second to billions of years. The half-life of uranium 238, which is used in nuclear reactors, is about the same as the age the Earth is now, 4.5 billion years.

A nuclear power plant in New York State. The reactors are housed inside the domes.

Fission and fusion

Nuclear reactors make use of the energy released by nuclear fission. This means splitting a large nucleus apart into smaller nuclei. When a nucleus splits, it releases a lot of energy. The fuel most often used in nuclear reactors is a form of uranium. The new nuclei formed when an unstable nucleus **decays** are called fission products. These new **atoms** are themselves unstable and will decay further.

As the uranium nucleus breaks apart it releases energy and two or three **neutrons**. These neutrons travel at around 20,000 kilometres per second and if they strike other uranium nuclei they will cause them to fission, too, releasing more neutrons. These neutrons can go on to strike yet more nuclei, which will release yet more neutrons, and so the reaction continues. This chain reaction is what makes it possible to obtain a continuous supply of energy from uranium. Within a typical nuclear power station there may be a hundred million million million fission chain reactions taking place at any time.

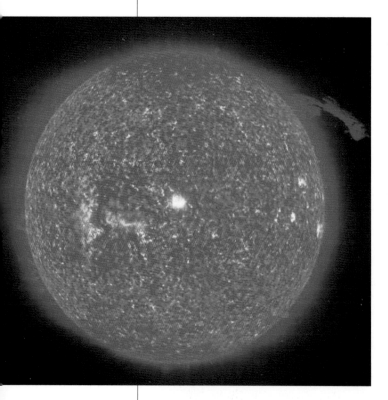

Critical mass

The minimum amount of a fissile material that can maintain a continuous chain reaction is known as the critical **mass**. Neutrons reaching the surface of a reactor core can leak out, rather than trigger further fissions. The smaller the core, the greater the proportion of neutrons that leak out. If the amount of fissile material is much greater than the critical mass, the reaction may accelerate uncontrollably. This is called a supercritical system and it is what happens in a nuclear explosion.

The Sun is powered by the same process as the hydrogen bomb. Millions of tonnes of matter become energy every second.

Nuclear fusion

Nuclear fusion is the opposite of nuclear fission. It is when the nuclei of two lighter atoms, such as hydrogen, combine to form a heavier one. The resulting atom has a smaller mass than the original ones, which means that some of the mass has been transformed into energy. This is the process that powers stars such as the Sun. Gram for gram, nuclear fusion produces eight times more energy than the fission of uranium, and over a million times more than could be obtained by burning the same weight of fossil fuels. Fusion is not only desirable because it is a wonderful energy source but also because the fuels used are relatively abundant and the product of the reaction is inert helium. However in experiments so far, the energy obtained in the laboratory has scarcely exceeded the energy put in to run the tests. Fusion reactions are difficult to achieve because a great deal of energy is needed to push the interacting nuclei together against the strong electromagnetic forces that cause them to repel one another. The nuclei have to be made to collide at very high **velocities** to overcome these forces and this requires heating to a temperature of 100 million°C or more.

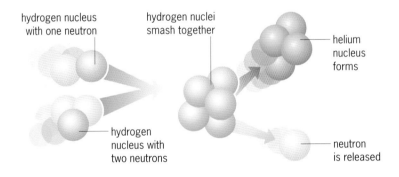

hydrogen nucleus with one neutron

hydrogen nuclei smash together

helium nucleus forms

hydrogen nucleus with two neutrons

neutron is released

Nuclear fusion is a desirable source of energy, but at the moment it is not economically practical.

Nuclear destruction

When a nuclear weapon detonates, most of the energy is released as intense **radiation**. This energy is absorbed by the surrounding air, creating a fireball that can reach temperatures of tens of millions of degrees Celsius. This burst of thermal radiation can cause severe burns on people several kilometres away and set light to houses, vehicles and forests. In cities firestorms can take hold. A shock front moves out from the explosion, followed by compressed air and strong winds of 500 to 1000 kilometres per hour, enough to destroy even concrete buildings. No one could survive this.

From nothingness to infinity

What we call the Universe is all of the matter and energy that exists and the space it occupies. Where did it all come from? The most popular theory at the moment is that the Universe came into being some fifteen to twenty billion years ago in a sudden expansion from a single point called the Big Bang.

Before the Big Bang, the 'Universe' was in an infinitely compact state, occupying a space smaller than the smallest atomic particle. Where did this come from? No one knows the answer to that question. For some reason this cosmic pinprick of energy began to expand. Within 10 microseconds of the expansion beginning, the first atomic particles had formed. It took half a million years for the temperature of the young Universe to fall sufficiently to let **atoms** form without being ripped apart.

Nucleogenesis

All the chemical elements were produced by **thermonuclear** reactions within stars, **supernovas** and in the Big Bang at the beginning of the Universe. This process is called nucleogenesis. As we have seen, inside a star, light nuclei are fused together to form heavier nuclei, and in this process **mass** is converted into energy in accordance with Einstein's formula, $E=mc^2$. These reactions are set off by the high temperatures and pressures at the centre of the star.

A star like the Sun has enough fuel in its core to burn at its current brightness for approximately nine billion years. A star that is twice as massive as the Sun will burn through its fuel supply in only 800 million years. A star that is ten times more massive than the Sun, burns nearly a thousand times brighter and has only a 20 million year fuel supply. On the other hand, a star that is half as massive as the Sun burns slowly enough for its fuel to last more than 20 billion years.

Birth to death, or rebirth?

According to the Big Bang theory, the Universe started from an instantaneously expanding point. Since then, the Universe has continued to expand, gradually increasing the distances between galaxies. The expansion of the Universe 'stretches' light rays so that blue light becomes red light. Thus, distant galaxies, which are rapidly moving away from us, appear redder. This is called the redshift. **Gravity** slows the expansion of the Universe. If the Universe is dense enough, the expansion will eventually slow down and reverse so that the Universe collapses in a Big Crunch from which it may expand once again.

Heat Death

If the density of the Universe is not high enough, the Universe will continue to expand forever. As a result, eventually all of the available energy will be evenly distributed throughout the Universe in the form of heat. As there will be no temperature gradient, there will be no chance of this energy being transferred from one place to another and so no work can be done. Effectively, nothing more will happen. This possible fate is known as the Heat Death of the Universe.

No end in sight as distant galaxies extend out further than we can see.

The minimum density that the Universe must have in order for it to stop expanding at some point is called the critical density.

Current evidence suggests that the expansion of the Universe will carry on at an accelerating rate. Across distances spanning the Universe, the force of gravity seems to be countered by another force, perhaps within the **vacuum** of space itself, that is pushing the Universe apart. Albert Einstein invented a term in his theory of relativity to prevent the Universe from collapsing in on itself and called it the cosmological constant. Although he later called it his greatest mistake, it appears now that the cosmological constant is real. Eventually gravity will lose – and the Universe will accelerate on into infinity.

Measuring energy

The system of units used by scientists is called the Système International (French for international system), or SI. These are units that have been agreed upon so that scientists everywhere can share their findings. The names of several of the scientists who investigated energy are preserved in the names of the units used to measure energy and its effects.

- The SI unit of energy is the joule, named in honour of James Joule, who demonstrated the relationship between **mechanical energy** and heat.
  1 joule is produced when a force of 1 newton moves 1 metre.
  1 joule is produced when an electric current of 1 ampere flows through a potential difference of 1 volt.

- The SI unit of force is the newton, named after Sir Isaac Newton, the English physicist who, among his many achievements, discovered the law of gravitation and set out his three laws of motion.
  1 newton of force causes a **mass** of 1 kilogram to move with an acceleration of 1 metre per second per second.

- The SI unit of power is the watt, named after Scottish engineer James Watt whose work led to the development of efficient steam engines.
  1 watt is the transfer of 1 joule of energy from one form to another in 1 second.

- The SI unit of temperature is the kelvin, named after Scottish physicist Baron Kelvin who developed the idea of **absolute zero** and invented a temperature scale based on this.
  1 kelvin is equivalent to a degree celsius in value.
  There are no negative values on the Kelvin scale, absolute zero being the lowest temperature possible.

- The SI unit of potential difference is the volt, named after Alessandro Volta, an Italian physicist who invented the first battery in 1800.
  1 volt makes a current of 1 ampere produce 1 joule of energy every second.

- ✔ The SI unit of electric current is the ampere, named after André Marie Ampère, a French physicist who studied electromagnetism.
  1 ampere is equal to the current that produces a force of 2 ten-millionths of a newton between two parallel wires 1 metre apart in a **vacuum**.

- ✔ The SI unit of resistance is the ohm, named after Georg Ohm, a German physicist who set out the relationship between current and voltage.
  1 ohm of resistance makes a potential difference of 1 volt produce a current of 1 ampere.

- ✔ The SI unit of electric charge is the coulomb, named after Charles Coulomb, a French physicist.
  1 coulomb is the charge delivered by a current of 1 ampere flowing for 1 second.

- ✔ The SI unit of **frequency** is the hertz, named after Heinrich Hertz, the German physicist who first discovered radio waves.
  1 Hertz is one complete vibration per second.

- ✔ The SI unit of radioactivity is the becquerel, named after the French physicist, Antoine Henri Becquerel, who discovered radioactivity in 1896.
  1 becquerel equals one radioactive disintegration (of an atomic nucleus) per second.

- ✔ The SI unit of pressure is the pascal, named after the French physicist, Blaise Pascal, who was the first to show how air pressure decreases with height.
  1 pascal is equal to a force of 1 newton applied to an area of 1 square metre.

Glossary

absolute zero lowest possible temperature, 0 degrees Kelvin (−273.15°C) at which atoms are in their lowest energy state

atoms smallest units of matter that can take part in a chemical reaction; the smallest parts of an element that can exist

carnivore animal that consumes other animals to obtain the energy and nutrients it needs

chemical energy energy held in the bonds that hold atoms together in molecules. Chemical energy is released during a chemical reaction.

chemical reaction when two or more substances (reactants) react together to form new substances

conductor material through which heat or electricity can move

consumer in the living world, herbivores and carnivores, animals that need to consume plants and/or other animals in order to obtain the energy and raw materials they need

decay the disintegration of the nuclei of radioactive elements

ecologist someone who studies the relationships between living things and their environment

electrical energy energy associated with the movement of charged particles

electromagnetic energy/radiation energy (including radio waves, visible light, X-rays and gamma rays) that consists of electric and magnetic fields moving together through space

electron one of the subatomic particles that make up an atom. Electrons have a negative electric charge and orbit around the central nucleus of the atom.

entropy the degree of disorder or randomness in a system

fluorescence light given off by a substance when it is exposed to radiation; for example, ultraviolet light

food chain feeding pathway along which energy and mass passes from one living organism to another

fossil fuels fuels produced through the action of heat and pressure on the fossil remains of plants and animals that lived millions of years ago. Fossil fuels include coal, petroleum and natural gas.

frequency number of vibrations or waves occurring within a stated time

friction resistance that one object encounters when moving over another

gravity force of attraction between any two objects

heat energy energy associated with the motion of atoms and molecules

herbivore animal that eats plants to obtain the energy and nutrients it requires

incandescence light emitted by an object as a result of it being heated

insulator material that prevents the passage of heat or electricity

internal energy the temperature of an object, which is the total of the potential and kinetic energies of its particles

ion atom that has gained or lost an electron and has an overall negative or positive charge

kinetic energy energy of movement

mass amount of matter in an object

mechanical energy measure of the amount of work an object can do; a combination of its potential and kinetic energy

micro-organism living thing that is too small to be seen with the naked eye

molecule two or more atoms joined together by chemical bonds. If the atoms are the same it is an element, if they are different it is a compound.

neutron one of the subatomic particles that make up an atom. Neutrons are in the central nucleus of the atom and have no electric charge.

nuclear energy the energy in the nucleus of an atom released when a large nucleus breaks down into two smaller nuclei (fission) or when two small nuclei combine to form a larger nucleus (fusion)

oscillate to move or swing backwards and forwards

perpendicular at right angles to a line or plane

photon particle representing the smallest possible quantity of light or other electromagnetic radiation

photosynthesis process by which green plants and some other organisms harness the energy of sunlight to make sugars from carbon dioxide and water

photovoltaic cell device that converts light energy into electrical energy

potential energy energy stored within a system because of its position or state

proton one of the subatomic particles that make up an atom. Protons are in the central nucleus of the atom and have a positive electric charge.

quantum quantity of energy corresponding to a single photon

radiant energy energy in the form of heat or light

radiation energy given off in the form of fast-moving particles or electromagnetic waves as a result of the decay of an atomic nucleus

reactant substance that takes part in a chemical reaction

solar energy energy from the Sun

subatomic particles particles such as protons, neutrons and electrons that are smaller than atoms

supernova star that suddenly explodes with a massive release of energy

thermodynamics study of the relationships between heat and other forms of energy

thermonuclear nuclear fusion reactions occurring at very high temperatures, as in the core of a star or in a nuclear weapon detonation

trophic level position occupied by an organism in a food chain

vacuum space in which no matter is present

velocity measure of the speed and direction of travel of an object

wavelength distance from one point on a wave to the same point on the next wave, for example from one wave crest to the next

Index